THE MAGIC OF THE BALLET

For Audrey and Ivy,
with lots of love
— V.F.

For Natalia,
with all my love
— L.O'H.

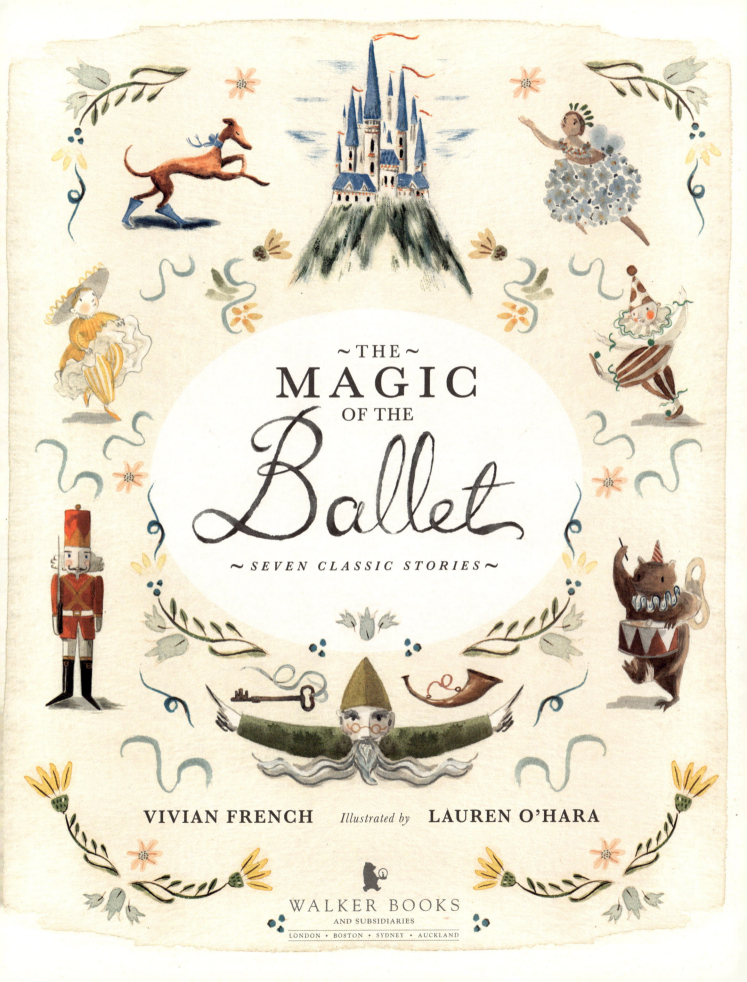

THE MAGIC OF THE Ballet

~ SEVEN CLASSIC STORIES ~

VIVIAN FRENCH   Illustrated by   LAUREN O'HARA

WALKER BOOKS
AND SUBSIDIARIES
LONDON · BOSTON · SYDNEY · AUCKLAND

INTRODUCTION

The lights dim, the curtains swish open, the first dancers float and shimmer onto the stage … and that's when the magic of the ballet begins.

I was around six or seven when I saw my first performance. The local ballet school was performing *The Nutcracker*, and I fell completely in love with the wonderful music, the enchanting costumes and, most of all, the thrill of a story told entirely through dance.

I decided then and there that I wanted to be a ballet dancer, and nothing was going to stop me. I ruined my new school shoes by trying to walk on my tiptoes like the ballet dancers did, and jumped and twirled until my mother finally got fed up and told me to stop – and I couldn't wait to see another show.

About half a year later, my grandmother took me to see *The Nutcracker* again, this time at a theatre … and I was shocked! The Mouse King I remembered had been turned into a scarily evil witch, and the dancing sweets were different too. I complained, and my grandmother explained that every ballet company presents the story in their own way, often to suit a particular dancer. She told me that the company we were watching had invited a very famous ballet dancer to join them, and they had changed the story to give her a new starring role.

Over the years I've seen all kinds of variations on the original stories, including a beautiful version of *Swan Lake* danced by a company of men. This made gathering up the stories for this book a problem, however. Which versions should I choose?

In the end, I decided to work closely from the plots of the ballets as they were first performed – and are, indeed, still often performed today. But there are plenty of modern choreographers and companies who have challenged the ideas that were acceptable in the eighteenth and nineteenth centuries, and quite rightly so. Maybe one day you, too, will change the ending of *Swan Lake*, or make sure that the characters in *La Sylphide* live happily ever after.

Whether you dance in *Coppélia*, watch a film of *The Firebird*, or go to the theatre to see *Giselle*, the details may sometimes be a little different from the stories in this book … but it will still, always, be magical.

CONTENTS

The Nutcracker 8

Swan Lake 28

Coppélia 48

Giselle 72

The Sleeping Beauty 90

La Sylphide 112

The Firebird 132

First performed 1892 in St Petersburg

Music composed by Pyotr Ilyich Tchaikovsky • Choreography by Lev Ivanov

Libretto by Marius Petipa

The ballet of *The Nutcracker* is inspired by Prussian author E.T.A. Hoffman's short story *The Nutcracker and the Mouse King*. Pyotr Ilyich Tchaikovsky was asked to write music for the show, and Marius Petipa was asked to adapt the story into the "libretto"; he was also due to "choreograph" the ballet (which means to decide the dancers' steps and moves), but after the tragic death of Petipa's daughter his assistant Ivanov took over. At first audiences thought the story – which was now much simpler and much less sinister than Hoffman's – was not serious enough, but gradually it has become one of the most popular ballets ever. Choreographers love to change the story, so there are lots of different versions.

Snowflakes were drifting past the window, but Clara Stahlbaum was too excited to take any notice.

She and her little brother Fritz were waiting on the stairs, watching the visitors arrive for the Christmas Eve celebrations and longing for the party to begin. Every year it was the same: no children were allowed in the drawing room to see the tree and the presents until all the guests had arrived.

"I do wish they'd hurry up." Fritz was wriggling with anticipation, and Clara put a soothing hand on his knee.

"It won't be long now," she told him.

One by one and two by two, the visitors' children came running to join Clara and Fritz – and there was soon a happy chatter as they tried to guess what each present contained.

"Tin soldiers!"

"A hoop!"

"A doll with a china face who can dance and sing!"

At last the doorbell was silent, and Fritz pulled at his sister's sleeve. "Clara? Clara! Can we go and see the Christmas tree?"

Clara held up a finger. "Just a minute ... look! Papa's closing the front door – everyone must be here."

Fritz jumped to his feet. "Let's go!"

All the children rushed into the drawing room. An enormous Christmas tree, hung with gold and silver balls and draped with glittering tinsel and scarlet ribbons, stood in front of the windows. Candles flickered and glowed on every branch, and at the top was an angel holding out her arms. Beneath the tree were parcels of every shape and size, and Clara's eyes shone as they saw them.

"Clara!" Her mother was calling her. "Clara! Your godfather, Herr Drosselmeyer, is here. Come and say hello to him."

Clara's godfather wore a tall hat and a cloak, and he walked with a cane; his eyes were very bright and he was interested in everything. Clara thought he might be a wizard, even though her father laughed at the idea – but Herr Drosselmeyer made such wonderful toys and games, she could never quite believe that he wasn't truly magic.

She was very fond of him, and she ran to greet him.

"I'm so glad you're here," she said, and the old man smiled.

"And I'm happy to see you, my dear Clara! Now ... would you like to see the presents I've brought with me?"

"Yes, please!" Clara hopped up and down in excitement, and Fritz and the other children came running to join her.

"Let me see, let me see." Herr Drosselmeyer snapped his fingers, and a servant brought in a big box. Eagerly the children opened it, and inside was a wonderful doll with eyes that opened and shut. When the old man lifted her out of the box, she began to dance – and the children gasped in astonishment.

Next was a doll of a soldier, and then one each of the much-loved characters Harlequin and Columbine ... and all were so lifelike, it was hard to believe they weren't real.

Once they had finished dancing, however, Clara's father took them away to keep them safe. "They're too precious for everyday play," he said.

Fritz came close to Herr Drosselmeyer. "Please – is there anything else?" he asked, and the old man smiled.

"Here!" And, much to Fritz's delight, he was given a pop-gun and a box of tin soldiers.

"Bang, bang!" he shouted. "I'm the captain of the army. Everyone get ready to march!"

As the children lined up behind Fritz, Herr Drosselmeyer pulled one last present out of his pocket.

"Don't think I forgot you, dear little Clara," and he gave her the parcel.

She tore away the wrapping paper, and discovered a wooden soldier doll with a big chin. "Thank you very much ... but what is it?"

"A nutcracker," the old man told her. "Look! You put a nut in his jaws, just like this, and CRACK! The nut's open!"

"Oh, I love him! I really do." Clara hugged her present. "He's much, much nicer than those dolls – I'll keep him for ever and ever!"

Fritz, leading his army round and round the room, saw that Clara had something new.

"What's that? I want it!" he shouted, and, rushing over to her, he grabbed at the nutcracker.

As Clara tried to push her brother away, the wooden doll fell to the floor and broke.

"Oh no, no, NO!" Clara burst into tears, and Fritz hung his head.

"I'm sorry," he said. "Don't cry so, Clara ... I didn't mean to break it!"

Still Clara went on crying.

Herr Drosselmeyer picked up the nutcracker and inspected it. "Easily mended," he said, and he wrapped his handkerchief round the doll's head. "Make him a bed, my darling girl, and tuck him in. He'll be as good as new in the morning."

Wiping away her tears, Clara began to make the nutcracker a cosy bed under the Christmas tree. Her father blew out the candles, and the visitors began to collect their coats – and their tired children.

"Thank you for a wonderful party," they said, "and thank you for the children's presents."

"Thank you for coming! We wish you a Merry Christmas." Clara's father waved the guests goodbye, then turned to Fritz. "Now you, my lad, can go straight to bed for breaking your sister's present."

As Fritz trailed away in disgrace, Herr Drosselmeyer kissed Clara goodnight. "Sleep well, my darling. I'll see you again soon." He bowed to Clara's father, flung his cloak round his shoulders, and disappeared from view.

Clara took one last look at her nutcracker doll, and then she too went slowly up to bed.

But try as she might, she couldn't sleep. Instead, Clara tossed and turned until at last she decided to creep back down the stairs, to see if her nutcracker soldier was safe.

It was very dark as Clara tiptoed into the deserted drawing room, and she hesitated in the doorway.

"Be brave, Clara!" she told herself, and she made her way across the room to where she had tucked her nutcracker into his little bed.

As she reached the Christmas tree the grandfather clock in the corner began to strike midnight, and she jumped.

"Oh!" As Clara gasped, the tree began to sway violently from side to side, and to grow up and up until it towered above her.

Her heart pitter-pattering in her chest, Clara turned to run – but a huge mouse blocked her way with an evil snarl.

This was the Mouse King: he wore a crown and a sword at his side. Behind him was an army of hundreds more mice, each easily as tall as Clara, and all scowling at her as they showed their sharp yellow teeth and dagger-like claws.

The Mouse King leapt towards Clara, and she screamed.

"Help! Somebody help me!"

"Everybody UP, then! Quick march! Left right, left right, left right!"

The tin soldiers jumped out of their box, and rushed into battle, guns at the ready. They fired their cannons, and sent shining sugar bombs flying through the air...

But although the mice squeaked and squealed, they continued their attack.

Clara put her hands in front of her eyes and trembled – until a voice shouted, "Have no fear! I am here!"

Peeping between her fingers she saw the Nutcracker, now grown into a tall soldier, wave his sword as he charged towards the Mouse King.

The Mouse King drew his own sword, and the two began to fight so fiercely that sparks flew in every direction.

Clara held her breath as she watched. Gradually the Mouse King beat the Nutcracker back towards the tree, and it became obvious that he was stronger. Every thrust of his sword was more vicious than the last, and Clara clenched her fists.

"That horrible mouse can't win… I won't let him!" And, pulling off her shoe, she flung it at the Mouse King as hard as she could.

"EEEK!"

Taken by surprise, the Mouse King froze. Only for a second – but it was enough for the Nutcracker.

"One two! One two! And here's for you!"

With one swift thrust of the Nutcracker's sword the Mouse King was defeated, and he fell to the ground.

There was dead silence ... and then the mouse army, heads bowed, dragged their leader away, never to be seen again.

"Thank you, dear Clara – thank you!" There was a flurry of snowflakes and, in front of Clara's astonished eyes, the Nutcracker turned into a handsome prince.

"I owe you my life," he said and, picking up the Mouse King's crown, he placed it on Clara's head. "Come with me, and I'll take you to a world of wonder ... the enchanted Land of Sweets!"

While the snowflakes whirled around them, a silver sleigh came gliding out of the shadows. They climbed aboard and, as the sleigh flew onward, Clara tried to catch the snowflakes – only to see them melt between her fingers. She laughed and the prince laughed too, and they were still laughing as the sleigh slid out into the sunlight, arriving in the Land of Sweets.

Clara's eyes grew very wide as she looked around. There were gingerbread houses with golden barley sugar twists either side of the doors, and fountains of lemonade; the ground was covered in sugar crystals, and the trees were hung with lemon drops. A twisting path edged with crystal bluebells led towards a pink and white marshmallow palace, and as Clara and the prince drew near, the Sugar Plum Fairy came out to meet them.

"Welcome," she said, and the prince bowed.

"May I present Clara, lovely fairy? She saved me from the evil Mouse King, and I owe her my life!"

The Sugar Plum Fairy held out her hands to Clara.

"How wonderful of you, dear child. Such bravery deserves a reward. While you rest, I'll ask my precious sweets to entertain you."

Clara was blushing as she sat down beside the prince, but she couldn't help feeling just a little proud of herself. She had never thought of herself as brave … but perhaps she was?

The Sugar Plum Fairy waved her wand: there was a flutter of feathers, and a flock of multicoloured birds came flying down to the lemon-drop tree and burst into song. The music was so cheerful that Clara couldn't stop herself from tapping her feet – and the next minute, the entertainment began.

Chocolate and Coffee were the first sweets to appear, but they were quickly followed by a host of others … so many that Clara lost count. When the Peppermints arrived, leaping and jumping and tumbling over each other, the prince stood up to cheer them on, but Clara began to worry that they must be feeling giddy. She was pleased when a group of

Marzipan Girls shooed the Peppermints away and performed a considerably quieter dance.

"Tweet, tweet, TWEET!"

A blue bird hopped onto a high branch, and fluttered his wings as if he was announcing something very special.

The bird chorus began to sing again, and Clara clutched at the arm of her chair as she stared at the next arrival. She had never seen anyone so tall, or with such an enormous skirt … and, as she stared, children came hopping and skipping out from underneath the skirt's silk petticoats.

"That's Mother Ginger," the prince whispered, "and those are all her children."

Mother Ginger called her children to her and swayed into the distance – and for a moment, there was a pause. The music stopped, and Clara held her breath until…

Sugared flower petals!

They came swirling towards the chairs where Clara and her prince were sitting and, as the music started once more, they lifted up their arms and began to dance. Round and round and in and out they floated, and the pinks and purples and blues and greens wove into ribbons and rainbows.

And then the birds fell silent.

"Is it over?" Clara asked.

But the prince put his finger to his lips.

"Shhh ... listen!"

And as Clara listened, slowly and sweetly, the bluebells began to ring out a tune. The flower petals drifted to one side, and the Sugar Plum Fairy came pirouetting out of her palace.

"She's so beautiful," Clara whispered to the prince, and he nodded.

The Sugar Plum Fairy was as light as thistledown; her feet hardly touched the ground, and Clara felt as if she was in an enchanted dream as she watched. When at last the fairy curtsied, and asked if she had enjoyed the entertainment, Clara's eyes were shining.

"When I grow up, I want to have a party that's just as magical as this has been," she said. "I'll never, ever, EVER forget it!"

"Clara ... look over there." It was the Nutcracker prince, and he was pointing to the end of the path.

The silver sleigh was waiting, and Clara sighed. "Is it time for me to go home?"

The prince smiled. "Yes, it's time now, Clara."

Clara sighed again. She kissed the Sugar Plum Fairy goodbye and, as she climbed into the sleigh, she looked sadly at the Nutcracker prince.

"And should I say goodbye to you too?" she asked.

THE NUTCRACKER

The prince shook his head, and jumped in beside her. "Never. I am your Nutcracker prince, and I'll always be yours."

He took Clara's hand, and the Sugar Plum Fairy waved as the sleigh carried them off and away.

On the way home, the sound of the tinkling bluebells echoed in Clara's ears. She closed her eyes to hear a little better and when she opened them again, she found she was safely tucked up in her own room, and the sun was peeping in at her window.

"My Nutcracker!" Clara jumped out of bed, and ran down the stairs. Into the drawing room she rushed – and there, under the tree, was her Nutcracker.

He was as good as new, just as Herr Drosselmeyer had promised … but one thing was different.

Now he was smiling happily, and right beside him was a bag of sugar plums.

THE NUTCRACKER

Petipa-Ivanov version first performed 1895 in St Petersburg

Music composed by Pyotr Ilyich Tchaikovsky

Choreography by Marius Petipa and Lev Ivanov

1895 was the first performance of *Swan Lake* as we know it. Tchaikovsky wrote the music in 1875 and it was choreographed by Julius Reisinger, who shortened the score and cast a ballet dancer called Pelagia Karpakova in the starring role. Karpakova added show pieces of her own, and the result was a failure. After Tchaikovsky's death, his music was revisited – and Petipa and Ivanov choreographed the ballet using the whole score. Pierina Legnani, an Italian ballet dancer, danced the Odette-Odile role and made *Swan Lake* famous with her 32 non-stop fouetté turns!

Swan Lake

"Happy birthday! Happy birthday!"

"Congratulations to our prince!"

"May you live long and be happy!"

"Best wishes indeed to Prince Siegfried!"

"Good luck to our future king!"

The lonely castle of Kiligartenz, home to Prince Siegfried and his mother the queen, was unusually busy. Every villager, young and old, had come up to the royal courtyard to celebrate the prince's birthday, and his friends had travelled from miles around to wish him well.

After all, this was no ordinary birthday… This was the prince's coming of age, and the day he became king!

Prince Siegfried's friends were especially delighted to see him. They crowded round, asking how he was going to mark the day, and what he was going to do in the future.

"Will you leave this lonely old castle?"

"Will you travel?"

"Will you still go hunting?"

The last question made Siegfried smile – he loved walking in the forests that surrounded the castle; forests that were home to dappled fallow deer, white-tailed rabbits, wild boar with curling tusks, and russet brush-tailed foxes. The trees stretched for many miles, and in among them were many beautiful glades that were dotted with yellow primroses in the springtime, and pink and white starwort in the autumn.

"Happy birthday, my dearest darling boy!"

The queen came swooping into the courtyard, and flung her arms round her son.

"Dear heart – I've been waiting for this wonderful day ever since you were born. Prince Siegfried: today you will take your place as the rightful king!"

"Thank you, Mother."

As Siegfried bowed, a page hurried out of the castle with a large parcel, and the queen presented it to her son.

"My gift to you on this most special of days," she said.

Siegfried ripped off the wrapping paper … and discovered a crossbow and arrows.

His mother smiled. "You and your friends can go hunting this afternoon. A last adventure – because tomorrow you will take up the responsibilities of the kingdom … and, of course, choose your bride."

"My bride?" Siegfried stared at the queen. "But I don't love anyone, Mother."

The queen frowned. "Siegfried! A king – and from tomorrow, you will be a king – has duties. One of those duties is to be married. I have invited the most suitable young women from our kingdom and beyond to attend your birthday ball tomorrow. I shall expect you to make your choice before the evening is over."

The queen swept away, leaving Siegfried clutching his crossbow and staring after her, his mind whirling. How could he possibly choose a bride out of these women he didn't know?

His friends, who had been watching and listening, laughed.

"You'd better make the most of today," they told him. "Let's go to the forest. You can try out your crossbow and arrows."

Siegfried had never expected that, in so little time, his life would change so dramatically. Heavy responsibilities awaited him … so perhaps his friends were right?

As he was wondering what he should do, a flock of swans flew over the castle in the direction of the forest, each swan's wings tipped with pink in the crimson light of the setting sun.

"Perhaps that's a sign," Siegfried told himself – and he led the way out of the courtyard.

At first, Prince Siegfried allowed himself to get caught up in the excitement of the hunt: the shouts of his companions, the baying of the hounds and the rush of wind through his hair as he galloped between the trees.

On and on he and his friends rode, always following the path of the white swans overhead – until, at last, the birds sank down and were gone from view.

By the time the hunting party had reached the heart of the forest, Prince Siegfried was no longer with them. Asking to be forgiven, he had ridden on ahead. He was happy to be alone; it gave him time to think about his future, and to wonder what would happen at his birthday ball.

What was he to do? He had to find someone to spend his life with, the queen of his kingdom … but how was he to choose?

The prince rode on more slowly, not caring where he went. His heart was heavy as he thought about the responsibilities that lay in wait for him as king: his childhood was behind him.

The sun was low in the sky and the shadows were growing longer when he found himself in a glade he had never seen before. To his surprise, he saw a reed-fringed lake in front of him, gleaming silver in the evening light.

The swans were floating peacefully on the water and, as Siegfried gazed at them, he saw one was wearing a golden crown.

Intrigued, the prince tied his horse to a tree and crept closer – never noticing the menacing shadow hidden among the reeds. The evil sorcerer, Von Rothbart, was crouching in the darkness … a creature half man, half owl. He was watching the swans with gleaming eyes and a triumphant smile.

Slowly, the sun sank into the blue-black clouds of night and, as the last rays faded the swans began to stretch their wings.

Siegfried caught his breath – was he dreaming? The swans were changing into girls … and the swan who wore the crown was the most beautiful girl he had ever seen.

As the prince stared at her, she stepped towards him.

"Please don't shoot us," she said. "We are only swans by day… At night we transform into the girls we really are." She put her arm round one of her companions as she pointed to the lake. "This is a lake of tears… The tears of unhappy parents, grieving for the loss of their daughters."

Siegfried shook his head in astonishment. "But how? Who are you? Who did this to you?"

"My name is Odette," the girl told him with a heavy sigh. "Many years ago my mother refused to allow a sorcerer with a cold and evil heart to ask for my hand in marriage, and he swore he would have his revenge. He cast a terrible spell on me and my companions… We are cursed to live as swans until the sun has set. At dawn we must become swans once more."

In among the rushes, Von Rothbart chuckled to himself. "Revenge is sweet."

"Can nobody break the spell?" Siegfried asked.

"We can only be free, and the spell can only be broken, if someone falls in love with me." Odette sighed again. "And not only must they fall in love with me, but they must ask for my hand in marriage … and never declare their love for another."

Siegfried listened intently. He had never seen anyone as beautiful as Odette, and at every word she spoke he became more and more certain that he loved her.

"I am Prince Siegfried," he told her, "and I never loved anyone before I saw you."

Odette looked at him, and she was very serious as she continued, "Be careful what you say, Prince Siegfried. If you break your promise to me, and tell any other soul that you love them, I will be a swan for ever and ever."

"I would never do that," Siegfried told her. "I love you, and you alone. My mother told me to choose a bride tomorrow at my birthday ball, and tonight –" he took Odette's hand – "I have found her. Come to the ball tomorrow! Please say you'll come!"

Odette smiled at the prince. "I'll come … just as soon as the sun has set."

As Siegfried kissed her, Von Rothbart rubbed his hands together in glee.

"Tomorrow will give me the chance for my final act of revenge," he muttered.

SWAN LAKE

He settled back to wait until the first light of dawn came slipping in between the trees. Then, his wings spread wide and his cruel eyes gleaming, Von Rothbart sprang out from the darkness of the reeds.

"Away with you!" he shouted. "Be swans once more! Away!"

Siegfried's arms were empty. A flock of swans circled above him, and as he stared up he saw the glint of gold on Odette's crown as she dipped her head in farewell.

The prince walked slowly home. All he could think about was Odette and, by the time he reached the castle, he saw that preparations had already begun for his birthday ball – and his heart leapt at the thought of seeing her again.

Brightly painted carts and carriages were rolling up the hill, bringing entertainers from all around the world, and guests were beginning to arrive from North, South, East and West – but Siegfried didn't give them a second glance. All he cared about was his beautiful Odette…

When the evening came, and the visiting princesses smiled and fluttered their eyelashes at him, he took no notice of them either. He was polite, but that was all.

His eyes kept going to the windows; was it sunset yet? When might he see Odette? When would she come?

His mother grew more and more impatient. "Siegfried! You know my wishes! You must choose a bride!"

"Not yet, Mother." Siegfried shook his head, and at that exact moment there was a crash of thunder, and the doors swung open.

Everyone stared as a tall and aristocratic nobleman strode into the ballroom, and Siegfried's heart missed a beat. A girl had followed the man.

"Odette!" The prince's face was alight. He was so certain his true love had come to find him that he leapt to take her in his arms, and sweep her onto the dance floor. He never noticed the nobleman's evil smile…

Because the girl was *not* Odette. She was Odile, Von Rothbart's daughter. The sorcerer had transformed her into the image of Odette, and he had turned himself into a member of the royal court so that no one would recognize him.

His smile widened as he saw Siegfried's adoring expression, and the way the prince gazed at the beautiful face in front of him – never once looking towards the window, where the real Odette was tapping frantically at the glass, desperately trying to catch his attention.

When the music stopped, Prince Siegfried held up his hand for silence. His mother and the court looked at him in astonishment as he stepped forward, Odile on his arm.

"Mother! My dear friends! I wish to make an announcement. I have chosen my bride – this is the girl I will marry."

Von Rothbart saw his opportunity. "Are you sure? Do you swear your eternal love?"

Siegfried drew himself up to his full height. "I, Prince Siegfried, swear on my honour that I will love her always."

"SO! You swear, do you?"

The sorcerer gave a shout of triumphant laughter.

"Then Odette is betrayed! Your promise is broken, and Odette is in my power for ever and ever and EVER!"

Before the horrified prince could speak, Von Rothbart had flung his cloak round Odile and the two of them swept away. Odette, watching from outside the window, gave an agonized, heartbroken cry.

"Betrayed," she whispered to herself, and then she ran back to the forest, weeping as she went.

Everyone in the ballroom began to talk at once, but Prince Siegfried didn't hear them. His heart pounding, he had only one thought in his mind.

He must find Odette, and tell her how he had been tricked – and tell her that he loved her, and her only.

Out of the castle he dashed, leaving his mother and all his guests staring after him. On and on he ran, until at last he reached the forest.

Von Rothbart, suspecting the prince might try to follow Odette, had cast a spell so that a storm whipped the trees into a frenzy, and tangled vines and sharp-thorned bushes blocked

the path, but Siegfried was not to be deterred.

Drawing his sword, he hacked his way through, until the shining waters of the lake of tears came into view at last.

Even as the prince had been struggling to reach Odette, her companions had been trying their best to comfort her.

"It was a trick," they said. "Siegfried will come for sure … just wait a little while."

But Odette was distraught. "I've failed you too," she wept. "We'll never be free of Von Rothbart's spell – never! And I'd rather die than live for ever as a swan."

As she spoke, Siegfried cut his way through the last of the twisted vines and came running into the clearing. He threw himself at Odette's feet, tears streaming down his face.

"I love you, and only you, Odette. The sorcerer tricked me. It means nothing – nothing at all. Forgive me! Please, please say that you forgive me…"

Odette stretched out her arms. "I love you too. And I forgive you, with all my heart."

"Then we'll be together for always," Siegfried told her. "My dearest, dearest Odette – from this time on, we will live happily ever—"

"STOP!"

The wicked Von Rothbart, dark wings outstretched, came hurtling down from the night sky above. Seizing Odette, he dragged her away from Siegfried, then drew his sword.

"She is mine! Mine for ever! Your words betrayed her, and my magic endures – and you, foolish prince… You must die!"

He leapt at Siegfried, his sword glinting in the moonlight.

As Odette watched, her eyes wide with terror, Siegfried defended himself from the sorcerer's ferocious attack. Back and forth they staggered as they fought, sparks flying as their swords clashed together – until Von Rothbart slipped and, for a second, the prince was free.

Seizing the moment, Odette kissed him … and then, convinced that death would be better than a life of enchantment under Von Rothbart's power, she sprang onto a rock and threw herself into the lake.

Siegfried saw her fall, and his heart broke in two. Life without Odette was worth nothing. With a wild cry, he leapt after her.

As the waters closed over the lovers' heads, Von Rothbart began to shiver and to shake. Defeated by the power of love, there was nothing he could do. His evil powers had left him.

Sinking to the ground, he dissolved into a heap of dark feathers as the sun rose, turning the blue lake into a sheet of shimmering gold.

Odette's companions, who had been watching in amazement, found themselves standing on the shore in their human form.

Not only had Von Rothbart been defeated, but his spell had been broken. As they greeted each other in delight, the beat of steady wings made them look up … and there, high above them, they saw two glorious white swans winging their way towards the distant hills.

Odette and Siegfried were together for ever.

First performed 1870 in Paris

Music composed by Léo Delibes • Choreography by Arthur Saint-Léon

Libretto by Charles-Louis-Etienne Nuitter

The first time *Coppélia* was performed, Swanilda was danced by Giuseppina Bozzacchi who was just sixteen. It was sometimes considered an unlucky ballet as, by the end of the year, France was at war with Prussia, Giuseppina had died of smallpox and the choreographer Arthur Saint-Léon had suffered a heart attack. In 1884, Marius Petipa restaged the ballet; Saint-Léon hadn't noted down his choreography, so Petipa wrote his own. Most productions now follow the 1884 version … and occasionally, Coppélia is played by a robot!

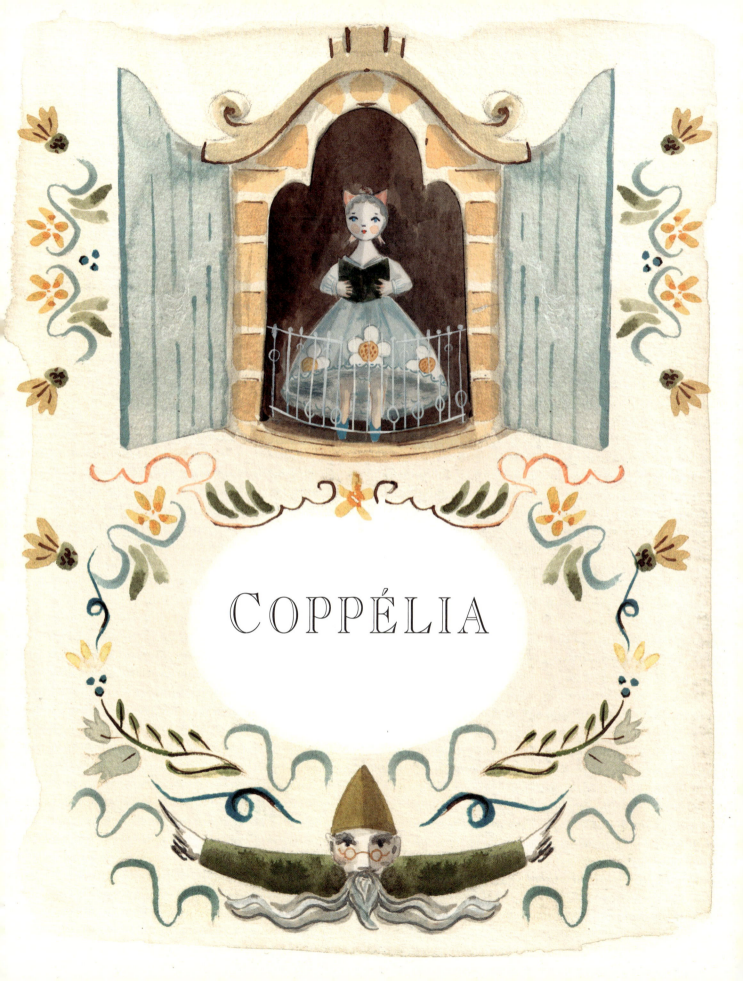

This story begins with a toy maker. He lived in a village on the very top of a mountain, and his name was Doctor Coppélius. Nobody knew much about him: he kept himself to himself, and this made him unpopular in a village where everyone liked to know everyone else's business.

People turned their backs on him, and talked together in low voices when they saw him walking by. "What does he do in that workshop of his?" they asked each other. "All that banging and clanging, and nothing to show for it!"

"Up to no good, I'm sure," said one.

"No good at all," agreed the rest, and it was decided that the toy maker was a highly suspicious character.

The children heard the grown-ups talking, and they ran away when they saw Doctor Coppélius.

The young people laughed at him, while secretly afraid of his gruff voice and fierce gaze and the strange noises that came from his workshop.

"I think he's scary," said Swanilda, who was the most beautiful girl in the village.

Franz, her sweetheart, put his arm round her.

"I'll protect you," he said, and Swanilda kissed him.

"Thank you," she said, and he kissed her back.

Doctor Coppélius pretended he didn't care what the villagers thought. He kept on working, day in and day out. He had spent the last months making a life-sized doll, and he was determined that she would be his finest creation ever.

Now, at last, she was finished.

Click, click, clickety-click… He wound her up.

Whirrrrr! Whirrrrr! Whirrrrr! She moved her arms and legs.

FLIP! FLIP! She opened and closed her big blue eyes – and the toy maker sighed as he looked at her beautiful face.

"I shall call her Coppélia, and she will be like my daughter," he told himself, and sighed again. "If only she were. A daughter would talk to me, and keep me company. It's a lonely life I lead."

A thought came to Doctor Coppélius, and he picked Coppélia up and carried her out to the little balcony at the front of his house. There was a chair there, and he sat the doll down and put a book in her hands.

Standing back to inspect his work, Doctor Coppélius actually smiled. She looked so lifelike that he almost expected her to smile back – but she didn't. Her eyes stayed firmly on her book.

"Enjoy the sunshine, Coppélia," the toy maker said, and he went back inside.

It wasn't long before the villagers noticed the beautiful girl on the balcony. "Who can she be?" they wondered. "Has Doctor Coppélius got a daughter? Has she come to visit?"

Swanilda decided she was going to find out. She went to stand underneath the balcony, and waved her handkerchief.

"Hello! Hello? My name's Swanilda! Let's be friends!"

But there was no answer. The girl didn't lift her eyes from her book; she went on reading.

Swanilda tried day after day to catch her attention, but nothing seemed to work. "Oh well," she decided at last. "She's obviously as grouchy as her father."

She was about to leave when she saw Franz coming towards her – but he wasn't looking in her direction.

He was too busy looking up at the balcony – and, as Swanilda watched in astonishment, he blew a kiss to the beautiful girl!

But she took no more notice of him than she had of Swanilda. She kept her eyes fixed on the book, until at last Franz sighed.

"I blow her a kiss every day, but she never seems to see me," he said, and he walked away.

Swanilda called to him and took his arm, even though her heart was very heavy. It appeared as though Franz didn't love her any more … and she couldn't help but wonder if she could go through with marrying him, or if she would end up alone for ever.

A band of street musicians was playing in the village square, and the young men and women were dancing as first Franz, and then Swanilda, came to join them.

Franz looked as if he didn't have a care in the world, but Swanilda was quiet. She was thinking about the girl on the balcony. Who was she? And did Franz really love her?

"Oyez! Oyez! Oyez!" The mayor came bustling out of the town hall. "Stop the music: I have news. And you, my dears, listen very carefully." He winked at Franz and Swanilda. "Our village has been given a wonderful new bell for our town hall. Tomorrow we'll be ringing our bell to celebrate all who are about to be married, and –" he nudged Swanilda – "I expect you and Franz will be there, Swanilda."

Swanilda didn't answer. How could she?

With a stifled sob she ran away, leaving Franz and the mayor looking after her in surprise.

It had been a busy day for the old toy maker, and now he was hungry. He moved Coppélia into his workroom, tucking her into an alcove behind a curtain before picking up his stick.

Then, after locking the door, Doctor Coppélius went out to buy bread and cheese … but as soon as he reached the village square a gang of boys came tumbling out of the shadows.

"Wooooooooo! Wooooooooo! Wooooooooo!"

They were hoping to scare him, but they only made Doctor Coppélius angry. He shook his stick at them, and chased them round the square.

"Be off with you, rascals! Can't you leave a poor old man alone?"

As the boys finally fled, Swanilda and her friends came running to see what all the noise was about.

They were just in time to see the toy maker marching off round the corner … but what was that lying on the ground?

"It's a key! It must be the key to the old man's house!"

Swanilda held the key in the air, and danced with delight.

"And he's gone for a walk – let's go and find that girl."

Her friends shivered. "No! It's too scary: there might be monsters!"

But Swanilda was determined to meet her rival.

"Well, I'm going to go," she said, "with or without you."

She ran towards the front door of the toy maker's house. The other girls looked at each other, and then, not wanting to be left behind, they tiptoed after Swanilda.

Carefully, carefully, Swanilda put the key in the lock.

Carefully, carefully, she turned the key … and then – CLICK! The door opened, and she was inside Doctor Coppélius' house.

Holding her breath, she crept up the stairs; her friends followed nervously behind her.

Little did Swanilda know that someone else – and someone very familiar to her – was also trying to get inside the house.

Franz had made his own plans: as Swanilda was sneaking up the stairs, he was carrying a long ladder across the square, planning to climb in the balcony window.

He was determined to meet the beautiful girl who sat there every day … and who wouldn't look at him!

Meanwhile, out on the landing, Swanilda's heart was beating fast as she peeped round the door – and then she gasped.

The room was full of people!

They were there in all directions, frozen into stillness. They weren't moving, or blinking, or even breathing.

"Have they been enchanted?" she wondered aloud. "Could Doctor Coppélius be a sorcerer?"

Creeping further in, she saw a velvet curtain drawn across a corner of the room.

Greatly daring, she twitched the curtain aside – and there, right in front of her, was the beautiful girl, still reading her book.

"At last!" Swanilda came closer. "I've come to meet you. What's your name?"

There was no answer.

"Why won't you talk to me?"

Swanilda came closer still.

"Don't you know it's rude to ignore people?"

There was still no answer.

"Boo!" Swanilda clapped her hands ... and then she began to giggle. Her friends, still huddled together at the door, stared at her.

"What's so funny?" a tall girl whispered.

"They're just dolls!" Swanilda came running back, pirouetting in delight. "Come and see." She went over to the nearest doll and wound it up.

CLICK, CLICK, CLICKETY-CLICK! The doll began to jerk its arms.

WHIRRR! WHIRRR! WHIRRR! Swanilda wound up another, and it kicked its legs.

T'RRRRK! T'RRRRK! T'RRRRK! A third nodded its head, and opened and closed its eyes.

With a whoop of joy, Swanilda's friends forgot their fears and ran to join in. They wound up every doll in the workshop, and jumped and hopped and danced among them.

They were making so much noise that they didn't hear when Doctor Coppélius opened the door, or see him staring at them in horror.

"Out! Out! Get out of here! How dare you?"

The toy maker rushed in, shouting and waving his stick, and the girls fled, shrieking and screaming as they went scurrying down the stairs.

COPPÉLIA

They never noticed that Swanilda wasn't with them. She had slipped behind the velvet curtain where Coppélia was sitting with her book – and she had just had a curious idea!

As the toy maker slammed the door shut after the girls, there was a scratching at the window. The scratching was followed by a screech, and the window was pushed open; a moment later Franz stepped over the ledge.

His eyes widened as he saw the dolls tumbled in heaps, but before he could go and look at them, Doctor Coppélius had caught him by the arm.

"What do you want, young man? Breaking into my home! Are you a thief?"

Franz hesitated, wondering what to say. He desperately wanted to meet the beautiful girl, but here was her father scowling at him.

"Please excuse me, sir! I wanted to speak to your lovely daughter. I saw her reading on your balcony, and my heart skipped a beat."

For a moment, Doctor Coppélius didn't answer. He was thinking. On his shelf there was a book of dark magic; a book he only dared to read at night.

It was full of spells and enchantments, and one in particular had fascinated him for years…

It was a spell that would take the soul from a real person, and turn his beloved doll into a living, breathing human being.

"If Coppélia were alive, I wouldn't be lonely any more," he thought. "I'd have a friend, a companion. I'd have someone to talk to, someone to look after me…"

He looked again at the young man, and did his best to sound welcoming. "Of course you shall meet her. My daughter told me that she'd noticed you."

Seeing Franz's face brighten, he added, "She often talks about you. But before I call her, let us have a glass of wine together. We can drink a toast to my daughter!"

Franz didn't hesitate. "Thank you," he said, and he threw himself into an armchair as Doctor Coppélius poured the wine.

He didn't see the old man slip something into his glass – but Swanilda, peeping through a hole in the curtain, saw everything.

Franz drank his wine in a gulp. "Now may I meet your daughter?" he asked.

Doctor Coppélius poured the wine a second time. "First: a health to my daughter!"

"Of course." Franz rubbed his eyes, then raised his glass.

"To the lovely … lovely … love—"

He never finished his sentence. He flopped forward onto the table, fast asleep.

The toy maker rubbed his hands together in glee, and hurried to fetch his magic book. Flicking over the pages he found the spell he wanted, and began to chuckle.

"At last! A soul for my Coppélia! I'll bring her to life! Now, let me see… *Ullaboo, hullaboo, gillaboo – ha!*"

And he began to mutter the words of the spell and wave his arms over the body of the sleeping Franz.

On and on went the spell, until finally—

"*HULLABOO* and *HA!*"

Doctor Coppélius ran to the curtain and pulled it back. Holding his breath, he held out his hand to the beautiful girl, not noticing, in all of his excitement, that his own doll had been swapped for Swanilda dressed as Coppélia.

"Come, my darling…" he said. "Come to me!"

The "doll" stared, then blinked her eyes.

She turned her head – and the toy maker gasped. He watched in awe as she moved first her hands, and then her feet. Slowly, slowly, she began to dance, stiffly at first, but gradually more and more easily.

"I've done it! Oh, my darling!" Doctor Coppélius rushed forwards, but the doll pirouetted away. Next minute she was whirling round and round, and as she twirled she knocked the magic book off the table and it fell to the floor with a crash.

"Oh no!" The old man ran to pick up his precious book, but before he could reach it the doll had sent the wine bottle flying, followed by a row of boxes from the shelves. Glass eyes, china heads, metal hinges, strips and springs crashed onto the floor and scattered in all directions, and still the doll whirled.

"Stop! Stop! My darling – please! Please! Oh … stop!"

The toy maker ran after her, pleading with her as she spun and spun, leaving chaos in her wake. She took no notice of him at all, until he sank to his knees with his head in his hands.

"Ruined! Everything is ruined!"

For a moment she paused, and as she did so Franz stirred, coughed, sat up, and rubbed his eyes.

"What's going on?" he asked. He rubbed his eyes again, and stared in astonishment. "Swanilda! Is that you? Why are you dressed like that?"

By way of answer, Swanilda ran to the curtain and pulled it back … and there was the real Coppélia, collapsed in a heap.

Franz's eyes opened wide. "She's a doll!"

"Exactly!" Swanilda was laughing at him. "You were blowing kisses to a doll!"

COPPÉLIA

"Oh." Franz blushed scarlet. "How silly am I?"

"Very silly indeed," Swanilda told him.

His blush grew deeper, and he hung his head.

"I don't deserve you," he said.

"No. You don't," Swanilda told him, but she kissed him – and then the two of them ran out of the door, leaving Doctor Coppélius weeping among his broken inventions.

It was the next day, and the village square was buzzing. Everyone was looking forward to hearing the new bell being rung for the first time, and to the celebrations afterwards even more. Franz and Swanilda were arm in arm, smiling at everyone; as their friends congratulated them, Swanilda curtsied and Franz bowed, while making sure he kept a tight hold of his sweetheart's arm.

"Dum, dum, dum-diddle, DUM!"

The band stopped playing, and the mayor came out from the town hall – but before he could begin his speech, there was a stirring in the crowd, and a figure came pushing and shoving his way through.

"Justice! I want justice!"

It was Doctor Coppélius … but he looked like a different man, with his face streaked with dust and tears.

"My whole life's work: destroyed! Broken! Ruined!" He pointed to Swanilda with a trembling finger. "It was her! That wicked, evil girl – she wrecked my workroom, and everything that was precious to me…"

The mayor frowned. "Look here, my good man! This is a joyous day – no time for complaints! Come and see me tomorrow—"

"No." Swanilda stepped forward. She was very pale, but her voice was firm as she said, "Doctor Coppélius is right. I *did* damage his workroom."

She gave Franz a sideways glance.

"I was angry; I thought he had a beautiful daughter who had stolen my Franz away from me."

She turned to the toy maker and met his eyes as she took another step in his direction.

"Please, Doctor Coppélius … let me pay you for what I did. I saved money for my wedding – but you shall have it all, every penny. It might not be enough, but it's all I have. And I'm sorry. I really, really am. Your doll was truly wonderful – a work of art."

The crowd began to murmur.

"So he makes dolls?" said one. "Why didn't he say?"

"And there was me thinking it was a real live girl on the balcony!" said another.

"He had us all fooled!" said the man beside them. "That was a proper work of art, and no mistake."

An old woman put out her hand and touched the toy maker's sleeve gently.

"Can you make another one? I'd surely like to see it if you did. I'd pay good money, too!"

Doctor Coppélius hesitated. For the first time in his life people were looking at him admiringly … and Swanilda's smile was warming his lonely heart.

"Perhaps I can pick up the pieces," he said gruffly. "I'll have to see."

Franz bowed. "I'd be delighted to help you, sir."

"Me too," said another young man, and his offer was echoed by other young men and women.

"Let us help!"

"Show us what you do!"

"So you'll accept the money I saved?" Swanilda asked. "Please?"

There was another pause, and then Doctor Coppélius actually smiled.

"No, my dear. Keep your money. But if ever you should feel like visiting a grouchy old man, I'll always be pleased to see you."

"Thank you! Thank you so very, very much!"

Swanilda flung her arms round the toy maker, and hugged him tight.

"I'll never forget you," she told him. "Never."

"Ahem." The mayor coughed loudly. "Let me assure the gentleman that, given the remarkable skill he has shown – not, of course, that I was fooled for a moment – I feel it only right that he is compensated for his losses by the village council."

The crowd clapped and cheered.

"In addition –" the mayor coughed again, and puffed out his chest so his chain of office glinted in the sunshine – "I declare Doctor Coppélius to be our National Treasure! And now: let the bell be rung, and our celebrations begin."

DING, DONG, DING, DONG!

COPPÉLIA

The great bell rang out, and everyone cheered. The band began to play, and Franz took Swanilda's hand.

"Have you forgiven me, my darling?" he asked. "And … may I have this dance?"

Swanilda laughed. "Of course, Franz," she said. "But I'll be dancing with you for the rest of our lives – right now, I'm going to dance with Doctor Coppélius!"

And to the old man's astonishment, Swanilda swept him off to dance round and round the village square until he was breathless … and very happy.

First performed 1841 in Paris

Music composed by Adolphe Adam • Choreography Jean Coralli and Jules Perrot

Libretto by Théophile Gautier and Jules-Henri Vernoy de Saint Georges

Giselle was a sensation when it was first performed, with Carlotta Grisi in the title role. It's still hugely popular: a romantic story with a haunting atmosphere, it demands tremendous skill from both the dancer playing Giselle and the one in the role of Myrtha, Queen of the Ghosts. In 1884 it was performed in St Petersburg and Marius Petipa added to the original choreography; we usually see his adaptation performed. Originally set in Germany, sometimes the location is moved to suit a new production.

In a pretty little village in the Rhineland, where geraniums bloomed at every window, a girl and her mother were arguing. The girl, who was named Giselle, had fallen in love with Loys – a newcomer to the village – and her mother didn't approve.

"Who is he?" Berthe, Giselle's mother, folded her arms, and glared at her daughter. "Where does he come from? He appeared out of nowhere, and nobody knows anything about him. I always thought you would be wed to dear Hilarion; we've known him all his life, and I know he loves you dearly."

Giselle glared back at her. "You can't choose who you fall in love with, Mother! I don't love Hilarion, and I do love Loys … and that's all there is to it."

Her mother shook her head. "But Hilarion is such a worthy young man."

"He's not the man for me, Mother!" Giselle stamped her foot. "He can't dance as well as Loys, and he's not nearly as handsome. Loys is everything I've ever dreamed of."

"Looks and dancing aren't everything," her mother told her … but it was no use. Giselle had made her decision: she believed that she and Loys were the perfect match, and nothing and nobody would change her mind.

Still, Berthe hadn't quite given up yet.

"Don't you know what happens to girls who fall in love with young men they know nothing about?" she said with a sigh. "They think they're going to get married, and live happily ever after – but the young men abandon them, and the girls die of a broken heart. And then –" Berthe lowered her voice to a whisper – "and *then*, their spirits become vengeful ghosts. Any man that walks in the burial ground in the forest is lured into dancing with them: dancing, dancing, dancing, until they die of weariness. Be warned, my darling!"

"Don't say such horrible things!" Giselle was furious. "Loys loves me, and I'll never, ever, EVER marry Hilarion!" And with that, she rushed out of the door.

As Giselle flung out of the house, she found Loys waiting for her. Music was playing to celebrate the end of the grape harvest, and all at once he swept her into a dance.

Looking up into his eyes, Giselle was sure he was her one true love. "Will I be your sweetheart for ever?" she asked, and Loys smiled down at her.

"For ever and ever," he told her with an answering smile.

Watching on from a little way away, Hilarion felt his heart sink. He stepped forward to see if Giselle would dance with him too, but she twirled off and didn't so much as glance his way.

"It's hopeless," he told himself, and he sighed heavily. "A stranger comes marching into our village out of nowhere, and steals my precious Giselle away from me. It's not fair!"

He stared at Loys despairingly – and as he did so, he began to notice something.

"He doesn't look like one of us," Hilarion realized slowly. "Those clothes he's wearing are satin and velvet!" His gaze sharpened. "And they aren't old and worn out like my clothes. He says he's a woodsman, but no woodsman I've ever met would be foolish enough to wear velvet. He's pretending to be something he isn't – I'm sure of it."

As Hilarion stood thinking, Giselle's mother came hurrying out of her house.

"Giselle, you'll tire yourself out! You're not strong enough, you know… You'll make yourself ill if you dance all day."

"Oh, Mother." Giselle shook her head. "I'm fine."

"That's what you think." Berthe frowned. "You don't look well. Come inside and rest." And she took Giselle by the arm, and began to pull her inside.

As she went, Giselle blew a kiss to Loys. "Until next time, my darling Loys – I love you!"

Loys simply nodded, and as the door closed behind his sweetheart he sauntered away… And as soon as he was out of sight, Hilarion seized his opportunity.

Hurrying to Loys' cottage, he checked to make sure no one was looking and then forced the lock with his dagger. Hearing the click, and hardly daring to breathe, Hilarion slipped through the door.

Once inside, there was very little to see: a few shirts were tossed over a chest, but that was all.

"It doesn't look as if anyone even lives here," he thought. "But what's in the chest?"

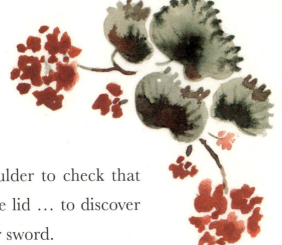

With another quick glance over his shoulder to check that he was still alone, Hilarion heaved open the lid … to discover a crimson velvet cloak and a gleaming silver sword.

"So: he's a humble woodsman, is he?"

Hilarion picked up the sword and inspected it.

"And what kind of woodsman has a silver sword with a crest on the scabbard? None that I know of!"

He tucked the sword under his arm and left the cottage, eager to find Giselle and show her what he had discovered – but the sound of a bugle made him stop, and step to one side.

A hunting party, led by the Duke of Courland, was riding towards the village green, and all the villagers came running out to stare.

The duke's ward, the beautiful Countess Bathilde, was among the party, and when they saw her beautiful clothes and glittering jewels, Giselle and her mother curtsied very low. Bathilde appeared to be amused by their admiration, and she stopped to smile at them.

Berthe was delighted to be noticed.

"Might we offer you some refreshment, my lady?" she asked. "My lemonade is famed throughout the land, and I would be honoured if you would accept a glass."

The countess nodded. "Thank you. That would be most kind." She leant forward, and patted Giselle's cheek. "What a pretty girl you are, my dear. Tell me, have you got a sweetheart?"

Giselle nodded. "Oh yes, I do, my lady … and we love each other dearly."

Bathilde's smile grew wider. "I too have a sweetheart – and quite soon, we are to be married. Isn't it the most wonderful thing, to be in love?"

"Yes, yes it is!" Giselle's eyes sparkled. "Truly wonderful!"

"And what do you like to do all day?" the countess wanted to know.

Giselle laughed. "Dance, my lady! I love dancing more than anything, and so does my sweetheart."

She looked over her shoulder for Loys, but there was no sign of him; with a shrug, she pirouetted round and round, and the countess and her courtiers clapped admiringly.

As Giselle sank into a final curtsey, Berthe came to say that the refreshments were ready. "And would you like to rest, my lady? You are most welcome to come inside."

The countess thanked her and accepted the kind offer, but the duke shook his head.

"We'll walk on a little further," he said, and he hung his bugle on the wall of Berthe's house. "Call me when you're ready to return to the castle," he added, and his companions strode away.

As Bathilde and her ladies followed Berthe into the house, Giselle saw Loys coming towards her. With a cry of delight, she ran to tell him how she had been dancing in front of a real live countess – but before she could begin her story, Hilarion stepped out from his hiding place.

"Look, Giselle!" He raised the shining sword. "This belongs to Loys … and no woodsman I've ever met has a sword like this." He swung round to the young man. "So: who are you?"

"What business is it of yours?" Loys was very angry, and Giselle took his arm.

"Go away, Hilarion!" she cried. "This is just your awful, awful jealousy talking!"

"Is that what you think?" Hilarion pointed to the crest on the sword. "Ask him about this!" He snatched up the duke's bugle, and held it out to Giselle. "See the crest on here? It's the same! He's a nobleman … there's no doubt about it!"

And before Giselle or Loys could stop him, he put the bugle to his lips and blew a long, echoing blast. At once, the door to Berthe's house opened and the countess hurried out. The duke and his companions came running back, and the villagers opened their windows to see what all the fuss was about.

Hilarion held the sword high in the air. "Admit it, Loys! Tell Giselle how you've been deceiving her!"

But there was no need for Loys to say anything. The countess had seen him and, as Giselle's eyes widened in horror, she held out her arms. "My darling Albrecht! My much-loved husband-to-be! What a pleasure … what a wonderful surprise!"

Giselle, trembling all over, looked first at Bathilde, and then at the young man she knew as Loys.

"Loys?" she whispered.

The young man sadly shook his head. "Albrecht. I am Count Albrecht. And I am promised to the Countess Bathilde."

With a wild shriek, Giselle's heart broke. Not knowing what she was doing, she rushed first one way, then another. Hilarion tried to catch hold of her, but it was a fatal mistake. Beside herself with grief, Giselle seized Albrecht's sword, and – with one last agonized cry – she plunged it into her breast.

There was nothing anyone could do for her: Giselle had drawn her last breath and, much to her distress, Berthe's prediction came true. Her daughter was buried in the graveyard in the forest, in a funeral attended by the villagers.

Nobody came from the castle. Word had come that Bathilde had told Albrecht that she would never marry him, and that she had left the kingdom for ever. She too was suffering from a broken heart … but nobody in the village wept for her.

Only Hilarion remained by Giselle's memorial stone after the funeral was over. As the evening shadows deepened, the forest grew dark and menacing – but still he stayed to keep faith with his love… Until faint wisps of silver mist floated in and out of the twisted trees. At first Hilarion took no notice, but as midnight struck the mist faded and he found himself surrounded by the spirits of the girls buried in the graveyard.

Their eyes burning and pale faces gleaming, the spirits surrounded Hilarion and invited him to dance – and he was unable to resist. He could see Giselle among the dancers, but she, too, was nothing more than a spirit now … and under the rule of Myrtha, the Queen of the Ghosts, who demanded complete obedience.

She had no power to help him.

"Faster!" the ghosts hissed. "Faster! Faster!"

And the unfortunate Hilarion whirled and twirled round and round and round, until he was breathless and dizzy – and *still* the ghosts made him dance. Round and round and round again…

Until he sank to the ground, lifeless.

Myrtha gave an eerie cackle of glee. "And so die all young men who dare to walk here! But come," she turned to Giselle. "I see another laying lilies on your grave. Do your duty, Giselle! Make him dance to his death!"

Her senses briefly returning to her, Giselle looked over to where Myrtha was pointing and saw Albrecht. He was kneeling beside her memorial stone, and weeping.

Giselle came closer, and with a cry of joy he jumped to his feet – but then stepped back as he realized she was a spirit.

"I loved you," he told her. "I loved you truly, and I will love the memory of you for ever and ever."

Giselle held out her hands to him and smiled her forgiveness, but the queen of the ghosts was without mercy.

"Make him dance! Make him dance NOW!"

It was impossible for Giselle to disobey Myrtha. She began to dance, but all the time she kept herself between Albrecht and the other ghosts, who were intent on revenge.

Albrecht was forced to dance too, and as the night wore on he began to tire and to stumble – but each time Giselle protected him, and danced his steps for him.

On and on crept the hours, and on and on Albrecht and Giselle danced.

The young count wept with exhaustion and begged to be set free, but Myrtha merely laughed, and urged him to leap higher and longer.

Still Giselle supported him … and the power of her love was so strong that the queen of the ghosts was unable to interfere.

At last, as Albrecht's breath came in painful gasps, the first light of dawn touched the tops of the tallest trees and turned them golden.

With a screech of frustrated fury Myrtha sank back into her grave, and the other ghosts faded into nothingness.

Albrecht leant against Giselle's memorial stone, hardly able to stand … but still alive.

With a sigh, Giselle put her hand against his cheek. "Thank you," she said. "Your love has saved me from everlasting torment as a spirit – and from now on, I will rest in peace. Remember me!"

And then she, too, was gone.

"No!" Albrecht stared wildly round, but all he could see was a rosebud lying at his feet.

Picking it up, he kissed it … and then walked slowly home.

First performed 1890 in St Petersburg

Music composed by Pyotr Ilyich Tchaikovsky • Choreography by Marius Petipa

Libretto by Marius Petipa and Ivan Vsevolozhsky

Ivan Vsevolozhsky, director of the Imperial Theatres in Russia from 1881–98, commissioned *Sleeping Beauty*. Under his instructions Petipa, the choreographer, worked very closely with Tchaikovsky, deciding how the story and music could work together. The first performance had a huge cast, and was set in the Palace of Versailles in the seventeenth century; it was very glamorous and very expensive, and partially designed by Vsevolozhsky himself … but all the Tsar of Russia could say was that it was "nice"!

Long ago and far away, when wishes were as common as butterflies on roses, there was a king and a queen who lived together in a castle with fifteen turrets.

They were very happy, because the queen had just given birth to a baby daughter … and they were both looking forward to celebrating her arrival with a magnificent christening party.

"The Master of Ceremonies has invited the Very Important Fairies," said the queen. "They'll bring our daughter wonderful gifts, and she'll live a long and happy life."

"What an excellent thought," said the king. "And how many fairies are there?"

"Six," the queen told him. "The Master of Ceremonies gave me the list this morning."

"Only six?" The king frowned as he inspected the list. "Are you quite sure? I had a suspicion there were seven Very Important Fairies…"

"The Master of Ceremonies told me six," the queen said. "And he never gets these things wrong."

"As you say, my darling," said the king. "And what are we going to call the baby?"

The queen smiled. "Aurora," she said, "because Aurora means 'dawn' – and our daughter will be just as beautiful."

The preparations for Aurora's christening kept everyone busy for the next few days. The six Very Important Fairies all accepted their invitations, and a royal feast was prepared.

At last the day came, and the king greeted their guests with a bow while the Princess Aurora kicked her little legs in the air and smiled.

The Very Important Fairies drifted down towards her cradle in a rainbow of colours, and the queen curtsied deeply as the first fairy – the Rose Fairy – stepped towards the cradle.

"I bring the Princess Aurora the gift of beauty," she said.

Next came the second fairy, who promised that Aurora would dance exquisitely well.

The third told the little princess that she would always be happy.

The fourth said that she would sing like a bird.

The fifth promised that she would also bring happiness to others.

"Thank you all," the queen said, and the king nodded.

THE SLEEPING BEAUTY

"Wonderful indeed!" And he took the queen's hand into his own.

There was still a final gift to be given: the last of the fairies, the Lilac Fairy, was the most beautiful of all.

She floated towards the cradle, her hands outstretched to bless the little princess with the gift of wisdom – but before she could say a word—

A *CRASH* of thunder!

A *FLASH* of lightning!

And the palace was filled with an ominous cloud of black smoke.

The courtiers and the visitors screamed, and the king and the queen stared in horror as a team of sharp-toothed rats came scampering into the palace, pulling an open carriage behind them.

Standing tall in the carriage, her black cloak billowing behind her, was Carabosse: the evilest fairy in all the kingdom.

THE SLEEPING BEAUTY

Her face was dark with anger, and her eyes flashed green as she towered over the cowering Master of Ceremonies.

"You forgot me! How dare you, you snivelling weasel of a man." And she snatched off the man's wig and hurled it to the ground. "Your royal master and mistress will pay for this … and they will pay dearly!"

Then, with a sneer, the fairy swung round to glare at the king and the queen. She pointed at the Princess Aurora's cradle.

"Look at this! A darling little baby – a baby that you dote on, a baby who has been given every gift she could possibly wish for. Well … I too have a gift for her. A gift you will never forget. A gift to remind you that Carabosse is never, never, NEVER to be forgotten again!"

The fairy's evil smile grew wider as she stepped closer to the cradle.

"The Princess Aurora will indeed grow into a beautiful girl, and she will sing, and she will dance, and she will be happy…

But on her sixteenth birthday she will prick her finger on a spindle, and DIE."

Carabosse threw back her head and gave an ear-splitting cackle of laughter.

The king and queen stared at her in dismay.

"No!" The queen stretched out her arms in entreaty. "Please, please – take this terrible spell away!"

"You shall have all the gold in the kingdom," the king promised, "if only you let our daughter live!"

"No, no, no, NO!" Carabosse laughed louder and louder. "I must have my revenge! The princess will prick her finger, and she *will* die."

"Just one moment."

It was the Lilac Fairy. She stepped forward from the shadows, and smiled at the frantic king and queen.

"Be of good heart, your Royal Highnesses. Remember – I still have a gift to give. I cannot undo Carabosse's spell, but I can soften it. The Princess Aurora will indeed prick her finger on a spindle, but she will not die – she will fall into a deep and peaceful sleep for a hundred years … and the spell will be finally broken when she is kissed awake by a handsome prince."

There was a moment of stunned silence. Then Carabosse, with a sudden and furious hiss of frustration, whipped up her team of rats and vanished from the palace. As she disappeared, the dark cloud lifted – and the courtiers began to tell each other what a lucky escape it had been for the princess and her parents.

The king and queen were shaking with relief as they thanked the Lilac Fairy over and over again, the baby princess held tightly in their arms … and the christening party began.

The years went by, and the Princess Aurora grew into a bright and beautiful girl, just as the fairies had promised.

The king and the queen made sure that she was never allowed near anything that might hurt her; all spinning wheels, knitting needles, sewing needles and pins were sent away from the palace.

But as the princess's sixteenth birthday grew near, the king and queen began to feel anxious again.

"We must hope for the best – and make Aurora's day the best it can possibly be," the king declared.

The morning of Aurora's birthday was gloriously sunny. One by one her friends arrived, and the palace became a hive of activity. Four handsome princes had travelled from far distant kingdoms in the hope of winning Aurora's hand in marriage, and the king and queen greeted each one, and made them welcome … but there was a sudden interruption.

THE SLEEPING BEAUTY

"LOOK! Knitting needles! Arrest them: throw them in the dungeons!"

The courtier had seen a group of country women chatting together, and knitting as they talked. The guards began to angrily hustle them away – how dare they bring knitting needles so close to the princess?

But the oldest woman ran to the queen, and pleaded for mercy with tears in her eyes.

"We're so very, very sorry, Your Majesty. We only wanted to share in the princess's special day, and we didn't realize what we were doing. Please do forgive us!"

The country woman sounded so genuinely sorry that the queen's heart was touched, and she took pity on her. "You may stay," she said, and the king agreed with her.

"After all, everyone wants to see our beautiful daughter," he said, and he smiled proudly as the Princess Aurora came dancing out to join her guests.

The four princes took it in turn to talk to Aurora, and to offer her flowers.

She curtsied, and danced with each and every one … but none of them were quite right. The first was too know-it-all, the second too aloof, the third had a sneering laugh and the fourth prince talked of nothing but horses.

When an old woman stepped forward from the crowd and presented Aurora with a pretty posy, she took it with a thrilled laugh. Waving it in the air, she danced away in delight – and nobody could catch her as she whirled and twirled, round and round. At last she stopped to look at the flowers more closely.

"What's this?" she asked. She pointed to something hidden among the petals, then gave a sharp cry of pain.

Her finger was bleeding.

"Her finger! She's pricked her finger!"

The whisper went from person to person as Aurora fell to the ground, and lay very still.

The terrified king and queen ran towards her, but stopped when the old woman threw back her hood and cackled wickedly. "What did I tell you? I am Carabosse, Queen of Evil! My spell has worked – I am revenged."

And with one last shriek of laughter, she disappeared in a cloud of choking smoke.

"Oh … my darling! My dearest!" The queen dropped to her knees beside her daughter, but as she took the princess's hand, the Lilac Fairy floated down and touched the queen's shoulder.

"Remember my promise, dear lady," she said. "The princess is only sleeping. She will sleep for a hundred years, and she will be safe and well for all that time, frozen as you see her now. When she is kissed by a prince, she will wake again."

"But how can we wait that long?" the king asked, and the Lilac Fairy smiled.

Without another word, she waved her wand … and gradually, one by one, everyone in the royal household felt their eyes closing. Their heads drooped, and they sank down onto chairs, or slipped to the ground.

Two minutes later, all that could be heard was the sound of gentle breathing and the occasional snore. The Princess Aurora, the king, the queen and every other person in the palace – young, old, and in between – were all fast asleep.

The Lilac Fairy waved her wand once more, and green shoots came springing out of the ground. Up and up they grew, until the palace was completely surrounded by a forest of sharp-thorned rose bushes.

"My work here is done," said the Lilac Fairy, "until one hundred years from now."

The years went by, and every year the roses grew thicker and stronger, but they never flowered. The Lilac Fairy watched and waited, and waited some more ... until, at last, one hundred years had passed.

Seeing buds appear on the rose bushes for the very first time, the Lilac Fairy flew over the hills and valleys to where a prince was hosting a hunting party.

Prince Florimund was everything his people thought a prince should be: modest and kind and good-looking. Everyone in his kingdom adored him, and tried their best to win his smile ... but he longed to find love, and to be happy. And no one he met seemed to be quite right.

Now, as the other members of the hunting party chatted and laughed and danced together, Florimund felt even more lonely. He wandered off into the forest until he could no longer hear the shouts and laughter of his friends, and sighed heavily.

"Will I ever find love?" he asked the trees. "Or will I always be as lonely as I am now?"

To his astonishment, he heard an answering sigh ... and a silver mist rose up from the ground around him. As he stared, the Lilac Fairy appeared and held out her hands.

"Dear prince, let me show you a vision that will cheer your poor sad heart. Watch – and be amazed."

THE SLEEPING BEAUTY

She waved her wand, and as the mist cleared the prince saw an image of Aurora as she had been on her sixteenth birthday, surrounded by her friends. Hardly daring to believe his eyes, he stepped forwards.

Aurora smiled at Florimund, and he caught his breath. She was so beautiful! Faint music from the hunting party came drifting through the trees and, his heart racing, the prince offered the princess his hand.

She hesitated, then took it – and they began to dance. As they danced, the prince grew more and more certain that Aurora was the girl he had always dreamed of. When her image faded away into the silver mist he ran after her, arms outstretched.

THE SLEEPING BEAUTY

"Come back!" he called. "Tell me who you are! Tell me where I can find you!"

But there was no answer, and instead he turned to the fairy. "Who was she?"

The Lilac Fairy smiled.

"That was the Princess Aurora," she said. "If you wish, I can lead you to where she is sleeping … but I should warn you that she lies under a spell. A spell that can only be broken by true love's kiss."

Prince Florimund clasped his hands together. "Dear fairy, I would cross seas and mountains to see her again! I love her! Truly!"

"Then come with me," the fairy said.

When Florimund first saw the rusted gates to the castle, and the tall stone walls covered in twisted and thorny rose bushes, he drew back in alarm.

"Surely no princess can be found here," he said, but the Lilac Fairy beckoned him on.

"Have faith," she told him.

And so he drew his sword to hack at the roses – only to find, to his astonishment, that the buds immediately burst into flower, and the tangled stems drew aside to let him pass.

"You see?" said the Lilac Fairy. "True love always opens the way. Now, follow me."

She led Florimund into the castle through a heavy iron door and, as the pair of them began to make their way through the corridors, the prince marvelled to see royal courtiers and servants slumped against the walls in every direction, and all fast asleep. Even the dogs were 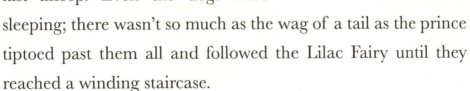 sleeping; there wasn't so much as the wag of a tail as the prince tiptoed past them all and followed the Lilac Fairy until they reached a winding staircase.

Up and up Prince Florimund climbed, with clouds of dust swirling about him and the wooden boards creaking underneath his feet.

At last he reached a room at the very top of the castle.

Slowly, ever so slowly, the prince opened the door…

And there was his princess, lying on a bed of silks and satins. She was very beautiful, and very still.

"Is she dead?" he whispered.

The Lilac Fairy shook her head. "The spell is heavy, but she only sleeps."

Hardly daring to breathe, Florimund bent over Aurora and kissed her lips. For a long moment he thought she wasn't going to wake, but then, with a cry of astonishment, the princess sat up and stared at the prince.

"I dreamed of you," she said. "We danced in the forest – and oh! It was wonderful!"

Florimund laughed. "It was indeed! Dear Aurora … I've loved you ever since we danced together. Will you marry me?"

The princess jumped out of bed. "Of course I will! But first you must meet my mother and father."

Hand in hand they ran down the stairs to where the queen was picking cobwebs out of the king's beard, and shooing mice away from her skirts.

"Mother! Father!" Aurora was alight with excitement. "This is the prince I choose for my husband – he came to find me, and to break the spell. He loves me, and I love him."

"Then we must have a wonderful celebration," said the king, and he sneezed. "Master of Ceremonies! Do your best. And first of all, please get rid of this dust!"

* * *

Every room in the castle was scrubbed and cleaned and polished, until not a speck of dust was left.

There were cooks working day and night, preparing cakes and pies and puddings, and a glorious wedding cake was carefully carried into the grand ballroom where the ceremony was to take place.

Thousands of red roses were gathered to decorate the walls, and as often as they were picked more grew until the sweet scent filled the castle and floated out to the world beyond.

The wedding day came: the sun shone, the skies were blue … and, out in the castle gardens, the birds were singing their hearts out, as if they knew it was a special day.

As soon as the royal guests had arrived, the Master of Ceremonies bowed to the king, the queen, the prince and the princess.

"Your Majesties! The entertainment is ready to begin!"

The king raised his hand in approval, and the Master of Ceremonies bowed a second time.

"Behold the world of Fairy Tale, for your pleasure and delight!"

First came a white cat, who danced with Puss in Boots and made everyone smile. Red Riding Hood was chased by the wolf, and a blue bird soared high to bring Aurora and Florimund good fortune and happiness.

At last it was time for Prince Florimund and Princess Aurora to exchange their vows. They stepped forward, hand in hand, and looked into each other's eyes.

"I love you," Aurora said.

"And I'll love you for ever," Florimund promised … and as he spoke, the Lilac Fairy fluttered down.

"My dear young people," she said, "I wish to give you one more gift. Your story will end as all good stories should. From this day on, you will live Happily Ever After."

The Lilac Fairy's wish came true. Aurora and Florimund lived happily for many, many years, and when their first baby was born the christening party had no unexpected visitors.

There was a rumour that the Lilac Fairy had put a spell on Carabosse's carriage so that she couldn't travel, but nobody ever found out for certain.

It was enough that she was never seen again … and that all had ended happily.

First performed 1832 in Paris

Music composed by Jean-Madeleine Schneitzhoeffer • Choreography by Filippo Taglioni

Libretto by Adolphus Nourrit

Marie Taglioni, the daughter of the original choreographer of *La Sylphide*, Filippo Taglioni, caused a scandal when she danced in the starring role – she shortened her skirts so the audience could see her legs! This was also the first time that a ballet dancer had truly danced "en pointe", which means to perform on the tips of your toes. In 1836, the ballet was re-choreographed by August Bournonville with music by Herman Severin Løvenskiold; it thrilled audiences in Copenhagen, and is the version most often performed today.

U p in the Scottish highlands – where tall pine trees whisper stories, and the north wind blows more often than the south – there was once a cottage.

It had belonged to Mrs Nora MacPherson and was now the property of her only son, James. Mrs MacPherson was a widow, and her one ambition in life was to see her son happily married to his sweetheart Effie; she counted the weeks and days and hours, until, at last, on a crisp autumn morning, the sun began to rise on James's wedding day.

The peat fire on the cottage hearth was burning brightly: the red and yellow flames danced in front of James's eyes as he sat and dozed in his armchair. He was dressed for his wedding but he had taken a moment to sit and dream.

LA SYLPHIDE

As he dreamed, the flames flickered and sank low. A curl of smoke rose from the embers … and James found he was looking at a silvery fairy, who danced through the smoke as lightly as a feather in the wind.

It was a sylphide!

James rubbed his eyes – and the sylphide vanished.

"Come back!"

The young man jumped to his feet, and stared at the glowing peat where she had appeared only moments ago.

Had he imagined the sylphide? Or could she be real? He had to know: his heart beat faster at the very thought of her.

"Come back! I want to see you again!"

The cottage door opened, but instead of the sylphide it was James's mother who came bustling in.

"James! Here's your darling Effie – she's wanting to know if all is prepared for the wedding?"

James blinked and pulled himself out of his dream. Effie had followed his mother, and he found himself comparing her bright blue eyes and rosy cheeks with the wonderful, ethereal beauty of the fairy.

Suppressing a sigh, he greeted both visitors with as much enthusiasm as he could muster.

"All's ready," he said, and his mother nodded her approval.

"Effie, my dear, does my James not look like a fine young man in his kilt and all? He'd be a grand husband for any girl!"

Effie blushed, and smiled at James. "I've been waiting for this day for a long time," she told him shyly.

James didn't answer. He was looking through the door, to where another young man was standing.

It was Gurn – and James frowned. Gurn had been James's best friend, until they had both fallen in love with Effie; when Effie had chosen James, Gurn had been heartbroken.

Now he had taken to following after Effie whenever he could, and James was growing tired of his friend's sad looks and heavy sighs.

"What do you want, Gurn?" James asked.

"Effie's friends are here," Gurn told him, and in came a group of boys and girls. They were followed by an old woman, who wrapped her grey plaid shawl round her shoulders.

She nodded to James, who felt he might recognize her, and then settled herself quietly in a corner to watch the wedding preparations; meanwhile, the girls chattered and giggled as they surrounded Effie.

"Are you excited, Effie?"

"Have you noticed how the sun is shining? That's a very lucky omen!"

"Who d'you think will catch your wedding bouquet?"

Effie laughed with them, and twirled herself round and round to show off her dress.

As she twirled, Effie caught sight of the old woman and she called out, "Old Madge! Old Madge! Come and tell us our fortunes!"

"Old Madge?" James stared as he realized who the old woman was. "How did you get in here? You're not welcome." He turned to Effie. "Don't you know she's a witch, Effie? She has evil powers!"

"Oh James, don't say that: she's a dear woman," Effie told him. "Be kind! All of us girls want our fortunes told, don't we?"

There was a chorus of agreement, and the old woman heaved herself to her feet, and came over to them.

"Are you *sure* you want to know, my pretties?" she asked.

"Yes! Yes!" The girls clustered round her, and Effie was pushed to the front.

"Read Effie's palm first, Old Madge!"

"Will she be a good wife?"

"How many children will she have?"

The old woman took Effie's hand in hers, and studied the palm.

When she didn't speak, Effie grew anxious. "What's the matter? Won't I have a happy marriage?"

Old Madge nodded. "That you will. I see a long, long life, with a loving and faithful husband."

Effie's eyes sparkled. "Did you hear that, James? We're to have a long and happy life together!"

"No, no, my dear." Old Madge shook her head. "'Twas not James I was speaking of. 'Twas Gurn that I see in your hand."

"What did you say, you wicked witch?"

James erupted from his chair, and towered over the old woman.

"That's nonsense! Get out of my house this instance!"

The girls pleaded with him to let her stay. "Please," they begged, "she's not told our fortunes yet!"

But James wouldn't listen to them. He snatched up a broom and used it to sweep Old Madge out of the door, before turning back to Effie.

"Don't believe her, Effie. Nobody can see such things in the palm of a hand. It's rubbish!"

"Indeed it is." His mother took Effie's arm. "Come away: you and your friends should know better than to listen to Old Madge. Your flowers are upstairs; follow me, and I'll braid them in your hair."

As Effie and her friends trooped off, James sat back down in his chair.

He stared longingly into the fire on the hearth; would the sylphide show herself again? The flames were flickering as if there were a gentle breeze in the room – and then there she was, standing in front of him! Weeping silver tears…

"What is it?" James asked. "Tell me: why are you crying?"

The sylphide shook her head.

LA SYLPHIDE

"You – the man I love – are marrying another. Alone, unloved and unwanted, I have nothing to live for. And so, I will die."

"But I do love you!"

As he spoke, James knew it was true. Overcome with emotion, he swept the sylphide into his arms and kissed her – never noticing that Gurn had come down the stairs, and was watching him all the while.

"James!" Gurn was horrified. "Whatever are you doing?"

Startled, James swung round; the sylphide slipped behind the curtain.

"Effie! Effie?" called Gurn. "Come here at once!"

A moment later Effie came hurrying down. "What is it? What's wrong?"

Gurn pointed to the curtain.

"James was kissing a fairy! I saw him! And now she's hiding."

Running over to the curtain, Effie pulled it back – but there was nothing there, and she laughed.

"I hope you're not jealous, Gurn," she said. "You seem to be imagining things!"

"I am not." Gurn scowled at James. "Ask him! Ask him if he loves you."

But Effie's friends were calling. Blowing a kiss to both Gurn and James, she hurried upstairs.

Before Gurn could say anything else, the priest and the fiddler were knocking at the door.

"Time for the wedding to begin," the priest declared, and at once the fiddler began to play "Flower of Scotland".

As the notes of the traditional wedding tune echoed through the cottage, Effie came slowly down the stairs again, her bridesmaids in procession behind her.

She went to stand beside James and took his hand – but to her surprise, he didn't look at her.

He was gazing at the glowing embers on the hearth, and it was very obvious that he was thinking of something other than his bride-to-be.

Effie glanced at the fiddler.

"Play a jig! My James is half asleep still … wake him up with a dance."

The fiddler changed to a tune that set the bridesmaids' toes tapping, and Effie swirled James into the middle of the floor. The music made everyone swing and skip, and even the priest took a turn with James's mother.

James began to smile, and Effie to laugh – but then, invisible to all except James, the sylphide slipped in to join the dancers, and her mournful silver eyes never left his face.

LA SYLPHIDE

"Ahem." The priest coughed, and the music stopped. "A most delightful entertainment! But now to more important matters. We must get ready to hear our young couple make their vows, the one to the other. James, do you have the ring?"

James, hardly knowing what he was doing, fished in his pocket and brought out a golden ring. As he did so, the sylphide swooped down and snatched it from his hand.

"Mine!" she whispered, and then she was gone, flying out of the door – and James, with a heartbroken cry, ran after her.

Tears streamed from Effie's eyes, and her guests wept in sympathy. How could a bridegroom abandon his bride?

"You're best off without him, my pretty." Old Madge was standing in the doorway. "You stay with the one as loves you true, and be happy all your days!"

She pointed to Gurn, and Effie threw herself into his arms for comfort.

James never thought of the misery he had caused; he could only think of catching his beautiful fairy. He ran and ran until each breath tore at his throat, but she was always just out of reach.

When he was finally forced to stop, she stopped too … but still beyond his grasp.

Other fairies came floating through the trees, glimmering in the dark shadows cast by the tall green pines; they circled round James, and watched him with cold silver eyes, but they never, never touched him.

Over and over again, James implored the sylphide to come to him – but she wouldn't listen.

Sometimes she beckoned, and led him further and further into the forest; other times, she vanished completely, only to reappear just as he thought he had lost her for ever.

It was at one of these moments, when the sylphide was suddenly nowhere to be seen, that he stumbled across Old Madge's hovel.

The old woman was stirring a cauldron in front of her door, and she greeted James with a cackling laugh.

"Looking for me, were you, young man?"

James, so desperate that he never noticed her sly expression, came closer.

"Can the sylphide ever become mortal?" he asked her.

Old Madge gave a dark chuckle. "Not so quick to call me names now, are you, laddie!"

"Help me!" James begged. "Help me, and I'll never call you names again!"

"So: you need a wood spirit to become flesh and bone?"

The old woman stirred her cauldron round and round as James stood watching her, hoping against hope that she could cast the spell he needed.

"Let me see, let me see."

She dipped a bony hand into the steaming liquid and pulled out a long lacy scarf, twinkling as if it had been sprinkled with stars.

"Here, laddie. Wrap it round your sylphide's shoulders, and she will be as human as you."

Hardly pausing to thank Old Madge, James seized the scarf and plunged back into the forest. Almost immediately, he was surrounded by fluttering fairies – pointing at him, and whispering to each other.

"Where is she?" he asked. "I've the best news of all!"

He punched the air in joy, and swung round to look for his love. As she came shimmering through the trees, James held out the scarf to her.

"I have a magic charm: you will be human! We can get married – we'll live happily ever after."

The sylphide floated down, her eyes very wide. "Is it true?"

James's smile lit up his face as he gazed at her. "It's true! Watch!"

With a twist of his arm he dropped the lacy scarf over her shoulders, and stepped back to watch the magical transformation from fairy to human.

There was no transformation. The sylphide cried out in agony, and sank to the ground before James's horrified gaze. Her companions rushed to support her, but when they lifted her up she was limp – and no longer breathing.

"Let me hold her! Please!" James was trembling, but they ignored him.

Carrying the sylphide tenderly in their arms, they drifted higher and higher into the air, and James was powerless to do anything to stop them.

As he stared helplessly upwards, the gold wedding ring slipped from the sylphide's finger, and dropped at his feet.

"Heh, heh, heh!"

Old Madge came through the trees: her eyes were gleaming, and she was cackling with glee, seeming more like an evil witch than she ever had before.

"So your pretty is gone! Gone for ever and ever! That'll teach you to call an old woman names, laddie, and to sweep her from your house as if she was nothing."

As James stared at her, she smiled wider. "Think twice, the next time you try to make a fool of an old woman who was doing you no harm."

She cackled again.

"Let's hope you've learnt your lesson, James MacPherson, or there'll be no luck for you. No luck at all."

James bowed his head. "I'm sorry," he said. "I truly am."

"Then you'd best hurry up and change your ways," Old Madge told him. "And now, listen!"

She held up her hand, and in the distance the miserable James heard the sound of bells.

Wedding bells.

"That's Effie wed to Gurn!"

James' heart was broken all over again, but Old Madge was jubilant and danced from foot to foot.

"A long and happy life she'll have," she told him gleefully, "and well deserved! Four strong sons and four fine daughters I see for her and her darling Gurn, and all loving and loved."

And then, with a final "Heh, heh, heh!" she was gone.

James stood very still, and his heart was very sore as he slid the ring onto his finger.

"Let it be a reminder to me to be faithful, from this day on," he whispered – and then he made his way home.

LA SYLPHIDE

First performed 1910 in Paris

Music composed by Igor Stravinsky • Choreography by Mikhail Fokine

Story from a traditional Russian folk tale

Commissioned by Sergei Pavlovich Diaghilev, founder of the Ballets Russes, this was Igor Stravinsky's leap into fame as a composer. The ballet company weren't so enthusiastic – they found his music difficult to dance to, and there were complaints and rehearsals up until the day of the first performance. Designers, however, have always loved *The Firebird*, and choreographers too; this ballet probably has more versions than any other ballet … perhaps because it comes from a traditional story.

Long, long ago, in a distant kingdom, there was a firebird. Nobody knew how old she was, but in the villages people said that their grandmothers' grandmothers had told stories about her, and it was well known that the firebird brought luck to everyone who laid eyes upon her.

If anyone was ever able to pluck one of her tail feathers, then that was very good fortune indeed, but she was so elusive that it was almost an impossibility. This had never prevented anyone from trying, however.

Prince Ivan was one of those people. He was young and handsome, but he had never found his one true love.

"If I were to own a feather from the firebird, then surely my life would change," he thought.

THE FIREBIRD

He asked all the travellers who passed through the kingdom where the firebird might be found. Nobody could tell him, until at last an old woman came to the palace selling firewood.

Prince Ivan, as always, asked his question … and for the first time, he was given an answer.

"She loves the golden apples that grow in the garden of the sorcerer, Koschei the Deathless," the old woman told him, and the prince's eyes lit up.

"Then that's where I'll go!" he cried. "Where is this garden, grandmother?"

The woman shook her head.

"You don't want to be going there, young majesty," she told him. "Koschei is evil, and he can't be killed. His magic is very strong: anyone climbing into his garden is turned to stone for ever and ever."

Prince Ivan put his hand on his sword.

"I am not afraid! I am Ivan Tsarevich, and I will find the firebird in this sorcerer's garden. Tell me where it is, grandmother, and I'll be in your debt for ever."

The woman sighed.

"Go five miles east of the Northern Mountains, then three miles south of the Western River. The garden is there, in the middle of the Dark Forest."

Prince Ivan bowed. "Thank you, grandmother. And I'll not forget you."

The woman sighed again. "You will if you're turned to stone, young majesty."

Prince Ivan set out the very next day. Following the woman's instructions, he went east and then south, and three days later he was rewarded by the sight of a castle surrounded by a high wall.

Tying his horse to a branch, he looked around; a tall tree caught his attention, and he climbed up until he could see what was on the other side of the wall – and his heart skipped a beat.

Drifting among the statues and flowers of the castle garden were thirteen princesses, and each princess was beautiful in her own particular way.

Twelve of the princesses were walking together, but the thirteenth princess walked alone. When she had drawn close to the wall, she looked up and saw Ivan.

As he gazed at her she blew him a kiss … and, at last, Prince Ivan fell in love.

He stretched out a hand to the princess, but she put her finger to her lips in warning, and the very next minute the hideous sorcerer Koschei came rushing out of the castle, growling and sniffing the air.

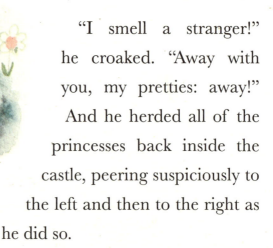

"I smell a stranger!" he croaked. "Away with you, my pretties: away!"

And he herded all of the princesses back inside the castle, peering suspiciously to the left and then to the right as he did so.

Ivan, who had pressed himself against the tree trunk so he wouldn't be seen, edged his way out again. The garden was empty, except for the stone statues … and, at the far end, a tree laden with golden apples.

"The golden apples!" Ivan's eyes shone. "If I can only catch the firebird, and beg a feather from her, I'll be lucky in love – and perhaps I can win the hand of the thirteenth princess!"

Desperate to reach the tree of golden apples, Ivan climbed higher, hoping to see a gate, but there was nothing. He climbed higher still, and then he saw it.

An oak tree had a branch that hung over the wall; from there he would be able to jump down to the other side!

At once the prince put his plan into action … and found himself among the statues.

Looking at them more closely he saw that they were all young men, their faces frozen in expressions of horror. A cold shiver ran down his spine as he turned away to hurry towards the tree of golden apples.

"Did they also come looking for love?" he wondered. "Did that monster of a sorcerer turn them to stone? And why is he keeping those princesses prisoner?"

As Prince Ivan reached the tree, he heard the faintest flutter of wings – and a glorious bird flew down on the other side of its branches.

Her body and wings shone with the glow of burning flames, and her tail feathers shimmered scarlet, yellow and gold.

Holding his breath, Ivan watched as she put her head on one side to inspect the apples.

"The firebird!" he whispered, and he crept towards her: one step, another, and another … and then, with a leap, he caught her by the tail.

"Let me go! Let me go!"

The firebird struggled and flapped her wings in Ivan's face, but he held on tightly.

She twisted and wriggled this way and that – but it was no good. She was caught!

At last, exhausted by her efforts, the firebird was still.

"Who are you?" she asked. "And what do you want?"

"I am Prince Ivan," the prince told her, "and I need one of your tail feathers to bring me good fortune … and love."

The firebird turned her head to look at him. "Love? You're looking for love?"

The prince sighed. "I am."

"And if I give you what you want, you'll let me go?"

"I promise," Ivan said, and he stepped away and put his hands behind his back.

There was a pause, and then the firebird bowed to him.

"I thank you for trusting me not to fly away. Here is a feather for you – and if ever you have need of me, just call."

She spread her shining wings, flew to the top of the tree and looked down at the prince.

"I wish you good fortune in your search for love."

And then, she was gone.

Prince Ivan was delighted. He tucked the feather into his cap, and leant against the tree of golden apples.

The sun was sinking low, and the evening star was twinkling in the sky as he gazed up at the castle windows, wondering where the thirteenth princess might be – and, even as he wondered, the castle door opened and all thirteen princesses came walking out.

Just as before, twelve princesses stayed close together, whispering and laughing … but the thirteenth went straight to the wall, and looked up to see if Ivan was still there.

"Princess!" Ivan called softly. "Princess!"

The princess heard him, and came swiftly over. "Who are you?" she asked. "And why are you here? Don't you know the castle is owned by an evil sorcerer? He'll turn you into stone if he sees you!"

But Prince Ivan could only think of her.

"I came to find love, Princess," he said, "and I have found you." And he held out his hand.

The princess looked over her shoulder at the castle, and shuddered.

"My companions and I are prisoners. We can never escape while Koschei the Deathless lives, and he can never die. So many young men have been lost already … so run, dear prince! Run away!"

Ivan shook his head. "While you are here, I will stay." And although the princess pleaded with him, he refused to change his mind.

As the evening turned to night, Prince Ivan fell more and more in love with the thirteenth princess.

She told him that her name was Katarina, and that she and her companions were seldom allowed out of the castle by day. At night the sorcerer slept – but he was surrounded by monsters who kept watch over the garden. If anyone tried to break in, or if the princesses tried to leave, the sorcerer was woken at once.

"So there's no way that you can rescue me," Katarina said sadly.

Prince Ivan took her hand. "Leave it to me," he said. "Tomorrow I shall ask the sorcerer for your hand in marriage. If he refuses, I shall run him through with my sword."

Katarina sighed. "But there's no heart in his body, dearest Ivan. He can't be killed."

COCKADOODLEDOO!

The sound of a cock crowing interrupted the princess, and she turned very pale.

"Koschei wakes at dawn, and I must be inside the castle walls! Don't follow me, my darling – if you do, it will surely lead to your death!"

She kissed Ivan.

"For my sake, please go!"

After one more kiss, she turned and ran into the castle.

Ivan took no notice of Katarina's warning. Drawing his sword, he hurried after her; the huge wooden doors had closed behind her, but he hammered on them.

At last, a fire-eyed monster peered out.

"What do you want?"

"I am Prince Ivan," the prince said, "and I demand to see the sorcerer Koschei! I have important business with him – the most important business in the world!"

The monster sniggered. "So you want to be turned into stone, do you? I'll see if he's awake."

Impatiently, Ivan waited. At last the doors opened again … and a crowd of hideous creatures came tumbling out, spitting and snarling and showing their crooked yellow fangs and curving claws.

Behind them strode Koschei, his eyes burning and his face dark with anger.

"Who are you, that dares to come knocking on my door?" he roared.

The prince bowed.

"I am Prince Ivan, and I am here to ask for the hand of the Princess Katarina."

Koschei drew himself up to his full height, and Ivan saw that he was trembling with rage. "Such impudence deserves the ultimate punishment! Look your last on the sun and the sky, foolish prince … for soon you will be *stone*."

The sorcerer raised his hand, and his creatures gathered round his feet, mumbling and dribbling in anticipation of Ivan's transformation.

"One moment!" Ivan pulled the firebird's feather from his cap, and waved it in the air. "I call upon the firebird. Firebird – I have need of you now!"

With a rush of golden wings the firebird appeared. She swooped over the sorcerer's head, and began to sing a song that made Ivan's feet itch to dance.

The hideous monsters were unable to resist the invitation; they lurched forward, and began to lumber round and round. Koschei himself swayed, and staggered from one foot to the other before he was driven by the magical music to join his creatures as they circled and spun.

Faster and faster they danced, while Ivan watched in astonishment: faster and faster and faster, until they were so exhausted that they sank down and fell into a deep sleep.

The firebird settled beside Ivan. He began to thank her, but she stopped him.

"Hurry to the tree of golden apples! Search among the roots, and you'll find an egg – and inside the egg is the heart of Koschei the Deathless. Break the egg, and he will die … but be quick! He's already beginning to stir."

Ivan, his heart beating wildly, dashed to the tree. Sinking to his knees, he tugged at the tufts of grass that grew at its base, and scrabbled wildly at the earth beneath, his breath catching in his throat as he worked.

"I can see the roots!"

He redoubled his efforts … and there, hidden deep under the tree of golden apples, was the egg.

Pulling it out with trembling hands, the prince jumped to his feet and hurled the egg to the ground with all his strength.

As it broke into a thousand pieces there was a piercing cry from the castle. Koschei was dead, and his hideous monsters were dissolving into mist.

"Ivan – my Ivan!" Katarina came running into the garden, and flung herself into the prince's arms.

THE FIREBIRD

She was followed by the twelve princesses who had been her companions, laughing in delight at being released from their captivity.

A moment later the statues began to quiver and shake – and where there had been twelve stone statues, twelve young men were standing.

As Prince Ivan and Princess Katarina left the garden hand in hand to live happily ever after, the firebird soared overhead in a celebratory circle. All was well, and she was satisfied.

There was just one last task. With a flutter of her fiery wings, she swooped down to the tree of golden apples. Now she could eat to her heart's content.

VIVIAN FRENCH writes in a messy workroom stuffed full of fairy tales and folk tales – the stories she loves best. She has retold classic tales in books such as *The Most Wonderful Thing in the World*, and has also created magical worlds of her own in her series with the artist Marta Kissi, including *The Wizards' Banquet*, *The Giants' Tea Party* and *The Dragon's Breakfast*. Vivian is the co-founder of the acclaimed Picture Hooks mentoring scheme for illustrators, teaches illustration students at the Edinburgh College of Art and is also a sought-after lecturer on the importance of picture books. She is one of the most borrowed children's authors in UK libraries, and was awarded an MBE for services to literature, literacy, illustration and the arts.

LAUREN O'HARA is an illustrator from the north of England. As a child she loved reading fairy tales, painting insects and listening to her grandmother's stories – she went on to study art and illustration at Kingston University, then designed window displays and props for films. Lauren's career as an illustrator began when she and her sister, Natalia, worked together on a picture book called *Hortense and the Shadow*, which was followed by three more books together: *The Bandit Queen*, *Frindleswylde* and *Once Upon a Fairytale*. Lauren has also collaborated with the author Sophie Dahl on her début book for children, *Madame Badobedah*, and has twice been nominated for the prestigious Kate Greenaway Medal.

First published 2022 by Walker Books Ltd, 87 Vauxhall Walk, London SE11 5HJ

2 4 6 8 10 9 7 5 3 1

Text © 2022 Vivian French • Illustrations © 2022 Lauren O'Hara

The right of Vivian French and Lauren O'Hara to be identified as author and illustrator respectively of this work has been asserted in accordance with the Copyright, Designs and Patents Act 1988

This book has been typeset in Baskerville

Printed in China

All rights reserved. No part of this book may be reproduced, transmitted or stored in an information retrieval system in any form or by any means, graphic, electronic or mechanical, including photocopying, taping and recording, without prior written permission from the publisher.

British Library Cataloguing in Publication Data:
a catalogue record for this book is available from the British Library

ISBN 978-1-4063-9876-2

www.walker.co.uk